UPTON SINCLAIR'S

# THE JUNGLE

ADAPTED BY PETER KUPER

**Dedicated to**
**The Workingmen of America**
-Upton Sinclair
**...and the Women too.**
-P.K.

**Also by Peter Kuper from NBM:**
ComicsTrips, $6.95
Eye of the Beholder, $10.95
Give It Up! and other Kafka short stories, $15.95
Mind's Eye, $11.95



ISBN 1-56163-404-2, clothbound
ISBN 1-56163-411-5, paperback
The Jungle adapted by Peter Kuper

Book Design by Peter Kuper
Printed in China
3 2 1

Library of Congress Cataloging-in-Publication Data

Kuper, Peter, 1958-
The jungle / Upton Sinclair ; adapted by Peter Kuper ; co-writer, Emily Russell.
p. cm.
ISBN 1-56163-402-2 (alk. paper) -- ISBN 1-56163-411-5 (pbk. : alk. paper)
I. Russell, Emily. II. Sinclair, Upton, 1878-1968. Jungle. III. Title.

PN6727.K67J86 2004
741.5'973--dc22

2004053095

ComicsLit is an imprint
and trademark of

NBM

NANTIER • BEALL • MINOUSTCHINE
Publishing inc.
new york

IT WAS FOUR O'CLOCK WHEN THE CEREMONY WAS OVER...
THE PLACE WAS THE REAR ROOM OF A SALOON IN THAT PART OF CHICAGO KNOWN AS THE "BACK OF THE YARDS." THIS WAS THE SCENE OF THE WEDDING FEAST AND THE JOYFUL TRANSFIGURATION OF LITTLE ONA LUKOSZAITE, WHO HAD JUST BEEN MARRIED TO JURGIS RUDKUS!

JURGIS CAN TAKE UP A TWO-HUNDRED-AND-FIFTY-POUND QUARTER OF BEEF AND CARRY IT WITHOUT A STAGGER. AND NOW HE IS AS FRIGHTENED AS A HUNTED ANIMAL.
ONA IS NOT QUITE SIXTEEN. SHE FLUSHES RED WHEN SHE SEES THAT JURGIS IS WATCHING HER.
HER COUSIN, MARIJA, IS SCOLDING AND EXHORTING EVERYONE WITH HER TREMENDOUS VOICE.
ONA'S BROTHER, STANISLOVAS, KEEPS RUNNING UP BEHIND HER, WHISPERING, BREATHLESS.
JURGIS'S FATHER, OLD DEDE ANTANAS, GIVES A SPEECH. ONCE HE WAS A SCHOLAR AND MADE UP ALL THE LOVE LETTERS OF HIS FRIENDS.
TAMOSZIUS PLAYS LIKE ONE POSSESSED BY DEMONS. YOU CAN FEEL THEM IN THE AIR AROUND HIM.
THIS MUSIC IS THE MUSIC OF HOME. CHICAGO AND ITS FACTORIES AND ITS SLUMS FADE AWAY. JURGIS AND HIS FATHER AND AS MANY ANCESTORS BACK AS LEGEND COULD GO, HAD LIVED IN THAT PART OF LITHUANIA KNOWN AS THE IMPERIAL FOREST.

JURGIS HAD NEVER SEEN A CITY UNTIL HE SET OUT FOR AMERICA. IF ONE COULD ONLY MANAGE TO GET THE PRICE OF A PASSAGE THERE, IT WAS SAID, HE COULD COUNT HIS TROUBLES AT AN END.
IT WAS IN THE STOCKYARDS THAT A FRIEND OF JURGIS'S HAD GOTTEN RICH, AND SO TO CHICAGO THE PARTY WAS BOUND. A FULL HOUR BEFORE THEY REACHED THE CITY THE GRASS SEEMED TO GROW LESS GREEN. THEY NOTICED A STRANGE ODOR, ALMOST RANCID, SENSUAL AND STRONG.
THERE'S A BOARDINGHOUSE NOT FAR FROM HERE.
SUCH WAS THE HOME TO WHICH THE NEW ARRIVALS WERE WELCOMED.
TOMORROW I WILL GET A JOB, AND THEN WE CAN GET A PLACE OF OUR OWN.

THE OFFICE.
KILLING BENCHES Nos. 3 & 4
THE NEXT DAY THEY SALLIED FORTH. THEY HEARD THE CATTLE, A SOUND AS OF A FAR-OFF OCEAN CALLING. THE MEN IN THE KILLING BEDS OF PACKINGTOWN WORKED WITH FURIOUS INTENSITY, LITERALLY UPON THE RUN. IT WAS THE GREATEST GATHERING OF LABOR AND CAPITAL EVER IN ONE PLACE. IT SENT ITS PRODUCTS TO EVERY COUNTRY IN THE CIVILIZED WORLD, AND IT FURNISHED THE FOOD FOR NO LESS THAN THIRTY MILLION PEOPLE!
SPEAK ENGLISH?
NO.
SEE DOOR? TOMORROW. SEVEN O'CLOCK. UNDERSTAND?
TANK ROOM.
CURING ROOM
POLISHING
CANNING DEPT. FILLING BY MACHINERY.

JURGIS WOULD NOT HAVE ONA WORKING. BUT MARIJA WAS NOT AFRAID OF MAN OR DEVIL. SHE MARCHED ABOUT UNTIL GIVEN THE CHANCE TO LEARN THE TRADE OF PAINTING CANS.
YOU'LL START MONDAY.
FIRE DEPARTMENT
LARD COOLERS, FILLING & COOPERAGE
SO THERE WAS ONLY DEDE ANTANAS.
FORGET IT, OLD MAN.
BUT WHEN HE CAME HOME HE SMILED BRAVELY, SAYING THAT IT WOULD BE HIS TURN ANOTHER DAY.
SOLDERING
LABELLING

THEIR GOOD LUCK IN FINDING WORK, THEY FELT, HAD GIVEN THEM THE RIGHT TO THINK ABOUT A HOME.
READ THIS
WHY PAY RENT?
YES, LADIES, THIS BRAND-NEW HOUSE WILL MAKE YOU A PERFECT HOME.
...RUNNING WATER, ALL NEW. KITCHEN...
WE NEED TO THINK ABOUT IT.
THERE'S ANOTHER COUPLE AND IF YOU WAIT TOO LONG...
HOW DO WE KNOW HE'S TELLING THE TRUTH?
WELL, HE HE DOES SPEAK LITHUANIAN...
IT WAS A FRIGHTFUL SUM, BUT THEN THEY WERE IN AMERICA, WHERE PEOPLE TALKED ABOUT SUCH WITHOUT FEAR.
$300 DOWN. SIGN HERE.
IT WAS HARD TO REALIZE THAT THE HOUSE WAS THEIRS. THIS WAS TO BE THEIR HOME!

A DELEGATE OF THE UNION CAME TO SEE JURGIS, BUT JURGIS HAD NO SYMPATHY WITH SUCH IDEAS--HE COULD DO THE WORK HIMSELF, AND SO COULD THE REST OF THEM, HE DECLARED, IF THEY WERE GOOD FOR ANYTHING.
BUT THERE WAS A CRACK IN THE FINE STRUCTURE OF JURGIS'S FAITH IN THINGS. HIS FATHER WAS FINALLY OFFERED A JOB--PROVIDED HE WAS WILLING TO PAY OFF HIS BOSS! IT WAS COMMON ENOUGH--PETTY GRAFT.
:cough:
...IT'S ALWAYS DARK AND THE HEAT'S NEVER ON... NOT A SINGLE DRY SPOT... THEY LEAVE CHEMICALS ALL OVER THE FLOOR...
THAT NIGHT, THEIR NEIGHBOR, GRANDMOTHER MAJAUSZKIENE, PAID THEM A VISIT.
THIS HOUSE IS UNLUCKY.
...AND BEFORE THAT IT WAS THE WOMAN OF THE FAMILY WHO DIED... AND BEFORE THAT THEY COULDN'T PAY THEIR INTEREST AND THE BANK TURNED THEM OUT...
INTEREST?
YES, HERE IT IS, OF COURSE.
BUT IT'S NOT FAIR.
WHAT DOES FAIRNESS HAVE TO DO WITH IT?
I WILL WORK HARDER.
WE WILL ALL HAVE TO MAKE SOME SACRIFICES NOW.

NOW THE DREADFUL WINTER WAS UPON THEM.
ONA HAD FOUND A JOB SEWING COVERS ON HAMS.
STANISLOVAS STOOD HOUR AFTER HOUR AT A LARDING MACHINE, MAKING NEVER A MOTION AND THINKING NEVER A THOUGHT, SAVE FOR THE SETTING OF LARD CANS.
DEDE'S COUGH GREW WORSE EVERY DAY. HE CLUNG TO THE IDEA THAT HE WOULD GET BETTER, AND GO BACK TO HIS JOB.
BUT AT LAST ONE MORNING...
AMEN.
YET THE GERM OF HOPE WAS NOT TO BE KEPT FROM SPROUTING. TAMOSZIUS HAD GOTTEN INTO THE HABIT OF VISITING MARIJA.
THERE WAS NO RESISTING THE MUSIC OF TAMOSZIUS.
ONE NIGHT HE FOUND THE COURAGE TO SPEAK HIS HEART.
MARRY ME.

Little by little, with each member working, the family gained a first-hand knowledge of the great majority of Packingtown swindles.
For instance, there was never the least attention paid to what was cut up for sausage. There would be meat stored in great piles in rooms, and the water from leaky roofs would drip over it, and thousands of rats would race about on it. The packers would put poison bread out for them, they would die, and then rats, bread; and meat would go into the hoppers together.
Jurgis was no longer perplexed when he heard men talk of fighting for their rights. Now he received the union delegate in a far different spirit.
Through the union Jurgis heard of Bubbly Creek. It was really an open sewer, containing all the drainage from the packinghouses. Here and there the grease had caked solid. An ingenious packer had begun to gather the filth in scows and make lard out of it.
Jurgis made sure every member of his family had union cards. He never missed a meeting, nor did Marija. She, too, had heard stories...
A butcher where she worked would describe diseased cattle covered with boils. Stuff such as this made canned beef.
Then there were the various afflictions of the workers. Worst of all were those who served in the cooking rooms. They often fell into the vats, sometimes being overlooked for days, until all but the bones of them had gone out to the world as Durham's Pure Leaf Lard!
The union made a great difference with Jurgis. He enrolled in a night school to learn English. He became a citizen and learned how to mark a ballot.

WITH SPRING CAME THE NEWS THAT ONA WAS WITH CHILD.
IF IT'S A BOY, WE'LL NAME HIM AFTER HIS GRANDFATHER.
BUT THE WARM WEATHER BROUGHT TRIALS AS WELL...
ONA'S BOSS WAS A MAN NAMED CONNOR. HE MADE FREE WITH THE GIRLS AT THE FACTORY. EVERYONE KNEW HE RAN A BROTHEL DOWNTOWN.
IT SEEMED THERE WAS NO PLACE IN PACKINGTOWN WHERE A PROSTITUTE COULD NOT GET ALONG BETTER THAN A DECENT MARRIED GIRL.
PUSH!
MISTER RUDKUS.
YOU HAVE A SON.
LITTLE ANTANAS!

CHILL WINDS BEGAN TO WARN THEM THAT THE WINTER WAS COMING ON AGAIN.
THE WINTER WAS A TIME OF PERIL. WHEN A STEER BROKE LOOSE THE ROOM WOULD BE SO FULL OF STEAM THAT YOU COULD NOT MAKE ANYTHING OUT. IT WAS IN ONE OF THESE MELEES THAT JURGIS TWISTED HIS ANKLE...
HE GOT HOME SOMEHOW, SCARCELY ABLE TO SEE FOR THE PAIN.
HOUR AFTER HOUR, UNABLE TO WORK, THERE CAME TO HIM EMOTIONS THAT HE HAD NEVER KNOWN BEFORE, AS IF HE WERE STALKED BY A GRISLY PHANTOM. IT MIGHT BE TRUE AFTER ALL, WHAT OTHERS HAD TOLD HIM ABOUT LIFE, THAT THE BEST POWERS OF A MAN MIGHT NOT BE EQUAL TO IT.
THE ONE CONSOLATION OF HIS LONG IMPRISONMENT WAS THAT HE NOW HAD TIME TO PLAY WITH ANTANAS.
ONA WAS GETTING PALER EVERY DAY, AND IT PAINED HER THAT JURGIS DID NOT NOTICE.
THEY WERE IN FOR A SIEGE, THAT WAS PLAINLY TO BE SEEN...

AT LAST, IN THE SPRING, JURGIS LACED A BANDAGE ABOUT HIS ANKLE AND RETURNED TO WORK.
WE GAVE YOUR JOB TO SOMEONE ELSE.
HE TOOK HIS PLACE WITH THE MOB OF THE UNEMPLOYED.
WE'LL TAKE YOU.
THEY WOULD STAND AROUND EACH MORNING UNTIL RUN OFF.
MOVE ON!
HE WAS SECOND-HAND, A DAMAGED ARTICLE.
THEY HAD WORN HIM OUT, AND NOW THEY HAD THROWN HIM AWAY!
THERE IS A PLACE THAT WAITS FOR THE LOWEST MAN...

THE FERTILIZER SOAKED THROUGH EVERY PORE OF HIS SKIN. THERE WAS A FRIGHTFUL PAIN IN THE TOP OF HIS SKULL. STILL, WITH THE MEMORY OF HIS FOUR MONTHS' SIEGE BEHIND HIM, HE FOUGHT ON.

ONA WAS PREGNANT AGAIN. BUT THEY RARELY SPOKE OF IT. THEIR MOODS SO SELDOM CAME TOGETHER NOW.
HE WAS WORKING IN THE STEAMING PIT OF HELL, DAY AFTER DAY. BUT FROM THE UNENDING HORROR OF THAT THERE WAS A RESPITE...
JURGIS DISCOVERED DRINK.
FREE LUNCH
ONA BEGAN TO FEEL THAT THERE WAS NO DELIVERANCE FOR THEM, NO HOPE.
IT SEEMED TO HIM THAT SHE HAD THE LOOK OF A HUNTED ANIMAL.

ONE MORNING SHORTLY BEFORE CHRISTMAS...
JURGIS, WAKE UP! ONA NEVER CAME HOME LAST NIGHT!
huh? WHAAA?!
ONA!
ONA!
ONA!
JURGIS!
JURGIS!
ONA!
WHERE HAVE YOU BEEN?
I-I HAD TO GO-- I--WAS--IT'S NOTHING.
I LOVE YOU!
WHAT ARE YOU SAYING?
OH JURGIS, BELIEVE ME-- THAT I HAD TO-- I DID NOT WANT TO DO IT.
HE MADE ME. HE WOULD HAVE RUINED US--HE...
WHO?! WHAT'S HIS NAME?!
WHO?!?!
MY BOSS!
CONNOR!

Midnight. Christmas Eve. In the distance a church bell tolled the hours.

BONG

Thirty days. Next case.

Ten thousand curses upon them and their law. His whole family might perish without him now.

BONG

He had been a fool! That he had nearly killed Connor would not help Ona.

BONG

He could not escape the vision that they would lose the house, after all their long, heartbreaking struggle.

BONG

Christmas Eve, but the bells were not ringing for him.

THE NEXT DAY, THE KEEPER LET IN ANOTHER PRISONER.
WHAT'S THAT DEVIL OF A STINK IN HERE?
ME.
WELL, IF IT ISN'T AN HONEST-TO-GOD WORKINGMAN. MY NAME'S DUANE. JACK DUANE.
THERE WAS THE TIME I...
JURGIS COULD NOT HELP LISTENING WITH WONDER TO JACK'S ADVENTURES AND PERILOUS ESCAPES.
MEET MY FRIEND, "THE STINKER."
HE MET PETTY THIEVES AND PICKPOCKETS, GAMBLERS AND FORGERS, OLD AND YOUNG. THEY HAD BEEN EVERYWHERE AND TRIED EVERYTHING. IT SEEMED TO JURGIS THAT THEY WERE WISE.
LOOK ME UP WHEN YOU GET OUT. MAYBE I COULD HELP YOU OUT OF A HOLE SOMEDAY.
IT WAS TEN DAYS BEFORE JURGIS HEARD A WORD FROM HIS FAMILY.
YOU HAVE A VISITOR.
STANISLOVAS!
...ONA LIES IN HER ROOM ALL DAY...
...MARIJA AND I LOST OUR JOBS BECAUSE OF CONNOR...
...WE CAN'T PAY THE RENT...
I-I CAN'T-THERE'S NOTHING I CAN DO.

HE COULD HARDLY BELIEVE IT WHEN THE TIME CAME. HE WAS A FREE MAN AGAIN.
IT WAS COLD, BUT ONCE HE GOT STARTED, HIS BLOOD WARMED WITH THE THOUGHT OF SEEING HIS FAMILY.
HE WAS HALF RUNNING AS HE ROUNDED THE CORNER. A SPASM OF FEAR CAME OVER HIM. THE HOUSE WAS A DIFFERENT COLOR!
WHAT ARE YOU DOING HERE?
THIS IS OUR HOME.
WHERE'S MY FAMILY?
I HAVE NO IDEA.
GRANDMOTHER MAJAUSZKIENE!! SHE WOULD KNOW WHERE THEY WERE.
THEY COULDN'T PAY SO THE LANDLORD TURNED THEM OUT. THEY'RE BACK AT THE BOARDING HOUSE.

JURGIS!
AAAAAAAA
IT'S ONA. SHE'S IN LABOR.
HURRY! WE NEED A MIDWIFE! HERE'S SOME MONEY. IT'S ALL I HAVE.
TAKE THIS, TOO.
MADAME HAUPT. COME QUICKLY. MY WIFE!
GOTT IM HIMMEL... VAIT!
VERE ARE WE GOING?
HOW MUCH YOU PAY?
THE NIGHT SEEMED ENDLESS.
I CAN DO NOTTING MORE. SHE'S DYING.
DER BABY IS ALREADY DEAD.
ONA! CAN YOU HEAR ME?! ONA!!
SUDDENLY HER EYES OPENED, BUT IT WAS ALL IN VAIN. SHE FADED FROM HIM. SHE SLIPPED BACK AND WAS GONE.

A MAN CANNOT STAY DRUNK FOREVER.
JURGIS! JURGIS! PLEASE COME HOME.
GO AWAY. LEAVE ME ALONE.
I BEG YOU. THINK OF ANTANAS.
MY SON...
FOR HIS SAKE...PULL YOURSELF TOGETHER.
I MISS ONA SO...I NEVER REALIZED HOW MUCH I LOVED HER.
AND SO HE WAS OUT BEFORE DAYLIGHT THE NEXT MORNING, HEARTACHE AND ALL.
WE NEED A MAN. WHAT'S YOUR NAME?
JURGIS RUDKUS.
RUDKUS? JURGIS RUDKUS? I WAS MISTAKEN. THERE'S NOTHING HERE FOR YOU.
HAVING ATTACKED A BOSS, HE STOOD AS MUCH CHANCE OF GETTING A JOB IN PACKINGTOWN AS OF BEING CHOSEN MAYOR. HE WAS BLACKLISTED!

THE ONLY THING TO DO WAS LOOK FOR WORK OUTSIDE PACKINGTOWN.
JURGIS PACED THE STREETS WITH HUNDREDS OF OTHERS, INQUIRING AT STORES, WAREHOUSES, AND FACTORIES FOR A CHANCE. FOR TWO WEEKS HE FOUGHT WITH THE DEMON OF DESPAIR.
IT WAS TOO FAR TO RETURN HOME EVERY NIGHT. HE WOULD CRAWL INTO A DOORWAY TO SLEEP.
THAT THE FAMILY DID NOT STARVE TO DEATH WAS DUE MOSTLY TO STANISLOVAS. IN A NEARBY DUMP HE FOUND HUNKS OF BREAD AND POTATO PEELINGS. ONE AFTERNOON...
YOU MEAN YOU'RE GOING TO EAT THIS?
TAKE ME TO YOUR FAMILY.
SHE WAS A SETTLEMENT WORKER. MARIJA WAS GLAD TO HAVE SOMEONE WHO WOULD LISTEN TO THEIR WOES.
TELL JURGIS TO TAKE THIS LETTER TO THE STEEL MILLS.
HE'LL FIND WORK THERE.
I PRAY THIS IS TRUE.
MAYBE OUR LUCK HAS CHANGED.

Hmmm, OKAY. WE'LL PUT YOU TO WORK ON THE RAILS.
IN TIME, JURGIS LEARNED HIS WAY ABOUT.
ANTANAS WAS REALLY JURGIS'S ONE DELIGHT IN THE WORLD.
ONCE MORE HE BEGAN TO MAKE PLANS AND DREAM DREAMS.
NOW THE SNOW HAD GIVEN PLACE TO RAINS AND THE UNPAVED STREET IN FRONT OF THE BOARDINGHOUSE WAS TURNED INTO A CANAL.
JURGIS WOULD HAVE TO WADE THROUGH IT TO GET HOME, BUT HE DID NOT MIND--IT WAS A PROMISE THAT SPRING WAS COMING.
WHEN HE SAW THE CROWD IN FRONT OF THE HOUSE HIS HEART STOOD STILL.
SOB
WHAT IS IT? WHAT'S HAPPENED?

ANTANAS IS DEAD. HE DROWNED IN THE STREET.
ANTANAS...
ALL AT ONCE A SUDDEN IMPULSE SEIZED HIM.
THERE WOULD BE NO MORE TEARS AND NO MORE TENDERNESS. HE WAS DONE WITH THAT.
HE WAS GOING TO FIGHT FOR HIMSELF NOW, AGAINST THE WORLD THAT HAD TORTURED HIM.

EVERY MILE THAT HE GOT FROM PACKINGTOWN MEANT ANOTHER LOAD FROM HIS MIND.
IN THE FALL JURGIS BID FAREWELL TO THE COUNTRY. ALL THE JOY WENT OUT OF TRAMPING WITH THE ONSET OF WINTER. HE SET OUT FOR CHICAGO AGAIN.

He began the long weary round of factories and warehouses.
Willing to work underground-- digging railroad tunnels?
Sure.
There would be falling rocks and crushed supports and premature explosions.
So it was that one day...
CLANG
CLANG
CLANG
When he opened his eyes again he was lying in the county hospital.

AT THE END OF TWO WEEKS HE WAS SENT OUT INTO THE STREETS.
UNABLE TO WORK, HE FELT LIKE A WOUNDED ANIMAL IN THE FOREST.
SALOONKEEPERS ALLOWED A MAN TO SIT BY THE FIRE FOR JUST SO LONG.
REVIVAL MEETINGS PROVIDED SHELTER, TOO, THOUGH JURGIS WOULD FEEL HIMSELF FILL WITH HATRED. WHAT DID THEY KNOW ABOUT SUFFERING? WHO BUT A FOOL COULD FAIL TO SEE THAT ALL THAT WAS THE MATTER WITH HIS SOUL WAS THAT HE COULD NOT FIND A DECENT EXISTENCE FOR HIS BODY?
AT THE END OF A WEEK EVERY CENT HE HAD WAS GONE. HE WAS FORCED TO BEG FOR HIS LIFE.
PLEASE SIR, I...
PLEASE, MADAME...
THEN LATE ONE NIGHT THERE BEFELL JURGIS THE ADVENTURE OF HIS LIFE.
PLEASE, SIR, I--
--I CAN'T WORK AND I'M HUNGRY.
POOR OLE CHAPPIE. BEEN UP--HIC!--AGAINST IT? ME, TOO. SHE'S A HARD OLE WORLD.
BETTER COME HOME AND HASSOME SUPPER WIZ ME. THASS THE TRICK.
TAXI!

HERE, OLE MAN. YOU PAY THE CABBIE.
I'VE GOT-- HIC! --NO HEAD FOR BUSINESS.
HIC... ZZZZZ.
HOW DO YOU LIKE IT, SPORT? MY OLE MAN'S PLACE. EVER HEAR OF JONES THE PACKER?
I...I'VE WORKED FOR HIM.
MASTER FREDDIE!
HAMILTON, MEET AN OLE FREN' OF MY FATHER'S.
HAMILTON, PAY THE CABBIE.
YESSIR.
BUT, I...

BUT SIR, YOUR FATHER... HE LEFT ORDERS.
WE'LL DINE IN HERE, HAMILTON.
PILE IN, OLE CHAPPIE.
MY FATHER'S OFF IN ITALY VISITING MY SISTER. SHE MARRIED A COUNT. MY BROTHER CHARLIE, HE... blah... blah...
LET'S GO...
GRRRR
...ZZZZZ...
YOU SON OF A...
OOF!

IN SPITE OF THE LAST HUMILIATION, HE HAD COME OUT AHEAD ON THAT DEAL!
SALOON
CAN YOU CHANGE A HUNDRED?
HOW THE HELL DO I KNOW IF IT'S GOOD OR NOT?
Hmmm. WELL, ALRIGHT. BUT YOU HAVE TO BUY A BEER.
25. 50. THERE. 95 CENTS CHANGE.
WHAA!? WHERE'S THE REST OF MY HUNDRED??
YOU'RE NUTTY.
MY MONEY!
HELP! POLICE!
MY MONEY!!!
WACK

WELL, IF IT ISN'T "THE STINKER."
JACK! JACK DUANE!
YOU WOULDN'T BELIEVE IT. FIRST I BROKE MY ARM IN THE TUNNELS. THEN THIS BARTENDER...
HARD LUCK.
THIS TIME LOOK ME UP WHEN YOU GET OUT.
AND SO, WHEN JURGIS WAS TURNED OUT OF PRISON...
I'M LOOKING FOR JACK.
IT'S SIMPLE, SEE. NOW ALL WE HAVE TO DO IS...
ON
WACK
DO YOU THINK HE'S ALL RIGHT? MAYBE I HIT HIM TOO HARD.
IT'S EITHER HIM OR US.

SUDDENLY, AS BY THE GIFT OF A MAGIC KEY, HE HAD ENTERED INTO A WORLD WHERE MONEY AND ALL THE GOOD THINGS OF LIFE CAME FREELY. ONE NIGHT JACK INTRODUCED HIM TO MIKE SCULLY, THE DEMOCRATIC BOSS OF THE STOCKYARDS.
WITH ELECTIONS COMING UP, I COULD USE A MAN LIKE YOU IN PACKINGTOWN.
I'M BLACKLISTED.
LET ME WORRY ABOUT THAT.
JURGIS CAME TO UNDERSTAND THE INS AND OUTS OF THE POLITICAL GAME. HE WENT FROM MAN TO MAN. THIS YEAR THE DEMOCRATS WERE PAYING FOUR DOLLARS A VOTE, THE REPUBLICANS ONLY THREE.
HE HAD NO IDEA THAT IT WAS SCULLY WHO WAS TO BLAME FOR THE UNPAVED STREET IN WHICH LITTLE ANTANAS HAD DROWNED, SCULLY WHO WAS AN OWNER OF THE COMPANY WHICH HAD TURNED HIS FAMILY OUT OF THEIR HOUSE.
TO HIM, SCULLY WAS THE BIGGEST MAN HE HAD EVER MET. HE COULD NOT GRASP THAT SCULLY WAS BUT A TOOL AND PUPPET OF THE PACKERS.

THAT MAY, THE CONTRACT BETWEEN THE PACKERS AND THE UNIONS EXPIRED. AN AGREEMENT COULD NOT BE REACHED. THE GREAT "BEEF STRIKE" WAS ON.
UNFAIR WAGES
THE PACKERS NEED MEN RIGHT NOW.
YOU MEAN CROSS THE PICKET LINE AND WORK AS A SCAB?
BUT JURGIS DID AS HE WAS TOLD.
THE PACKERS BROUGHT IN MEN FROM THE DEEP SOUTH, PROMISING THEM FIVE DOLLARS A DAY AND BOARD--AND BEING CAREFUL NOT TO MENTION THERE WAS A STRIKE.
JURGIS WAS SOON GIVEN A PROMOTION. AT LAST, HE WAS TO BE A BOSS!
HE GOT USED TO IT QUICKLY ENOUGH. HE STORMED AND CURSED AND DROVE THE MEN UNTIL THEY WERE READY TO DROP.
ONE DAY SOME CATTLE ESCAPED FROM THE YARDS. JURGIS AND HIS GANG WERE SENT OUTSIDE TO BRING BACK THE ANIMALS. BUT THE STRIKERS HAD GOTTEN HOLD OF THEM.
RIOT!

LIFE IS A CONTEST. HERE WERE TWO OPPOSING FORCES, TWO ARMIES. HERE WERE AGELONG WONDERS STRUGGLING TO BE BORN.

THE STRIKERS WERE OUTNUMBERED. THEY COULD NOT WIN THIS BATTLE, BUT THEY WOULD PUT UP A FIGHT. THE DREAM OF RESISTANCE HAUNTS A PERSON, HOPE CONTENDING WITH FEAR, UNTIL SUDDENLY A FETTER SNAPS--THE DREAM BECOMES AN ACT!

LET'S GET OUT OF HERE. THE COPS'LL FINISH UP.
JURGIS DESPISED WHAT HE'D DONE. HE WAS NOTHING BUT A SCAB, AN AGENT OF THE PACKERS. HE DRANK AND GAMBLED TO CONSOLE HIMSELF.
C'MON, LOVE. I'LL HELP YOU FORGET YOUR TROUBLES.
TAKE HIM TO ROOM #3.
CONNOR!
IT WAS THE MAN WHO HAD SEDUCED ONA, WRECKED HIS HOME, RUINED HIS LIFE.

HE CALLED ON SCULLY FOR HELP.
WHAT HAPPENED?
THIS GUY... CONNOR...A FIGHT.
PHIL CONNOR!? GET OUT OF PACKINGTOWN AS SOON AS YOU CAN!
YOU GOT ANY MONEY?
THIS IS IT.
AS A FAVOR, I'LL SETTLE THINGS WITH THE JUDGE.
LITTLE DID JURGIS KNOW THAT SCULLY WOULD KEEP THE MONEY HIMSELF.
BROKE ONCE AGAIN, JURGIS WAS AN OUTCAST AND A TRAMP.
IN ONE KIND OF PRISON THE MAN IS BEHIND BARS, AND EVERYTHING THAT HE DESIRES IS OUTSIDE.
IN ANOTHER KIND THE THINGS ARE BEHIND THE BARS, AND THE MAN CAN'T GET IN.

FINALLY, JURGIS WAS FACED WITH STARVATION.
HEY, YOU! STOP! COME BACK HERE!
RAAAH!
IT WAS SOME KIND OF RALLY.
A CHANCE FOR A FEW HOURS OF SHELTER AND WARMTH.
ZZZ...
OUT YOU GO, YOU BUM!
JURGIS? IS THAT YOU? JURGIS RUDKUS?

WHAT IN THE WORLD...?
I-I'VE HAD A RUN OF BAD LUCK.
I HAVEN'T ANY MONEY, BUT I CAN TELL YOU WHERE MARIJA LIVES.
MARIJA!
THE NEXT DAY...
I'M LOOKING FOR MARIJA.
WELL...
WHO IS IT?
WHAT DO YOU...
JURGIS!
I THOUGHT I'D NEVER SEE YOU AGAIN.

BUT... HOW COULD YOU?... A PLACE LIKE THIS.
MOST OF US HERE ARE DECENT WOMEN. BUT WHEN PEOPLE ARE STARVING THEY SELL WHAT THEY HAVE.
WHAT ABOUT TAMOSZIUS? DOES HE KNOW?
HE LOST A FINGER TO BLOOD POISONING AND COULDN'T PLAY THE VIOLIN ANYMORE. HE JUST DISAPPEARED.
AND STANISLOVAS?
"HE WAS HIRED TO FETCH BEER FOR MEN IN A FACTORY.
"ONE DAY HE DRANK TOO MUCH OF IT HIMSELF. HE FELL ASLEEP IN A CORNER AND GOT LOCKED INTO THE PLACE OVERNIGHT.
"WHEN THEY FOUND HIM THE NEXT DAY, RATS HAD EATEN HIM UP."
YOU MUST THINK I'M TERRIBLE FOR RUNNING AWAY.
NO. YOU DID YOUR BEST. THE JOB WAS JUST TOO MUCH.
WHO KNOWS? MAYBE IT WOULD HAVE BEEN BETTER IF ONA HAD KEPT ON WORKING FOR CONNOR. SHE COULD HAVE SUPPORTED US ALL.
YOU'VE GOT A CUSTOMER!
YOU MUST GO. BUT HERE'S SOME MONEY.
I DON'T KNOW WHAT TO SAY...

Jurgis could not get over the shock of all that Marija had told him.
Memories stirred that had been sleeping so long he had counted them dead. It had been the task of his recent life to fight them down, but now they overwhelmed him.
He thought of Antanas, whom he had meant to make a man. He thought of his father, who had blessed them all. He thought of Ona and their love.
His old ghosts beckoned to him. He heard the old voices of his soul.
RAAAH...

ANOTHER RALLY. REMEMBERING HIS TREATMENT OF THE NIGHT BEFORE, HE HESITATED. BUT IT WAS SO COLD OUTSIDE...
RAAAH...
SOCIALIS
TRY AS HE MIGHT TO STAY AWAKE...
HE SAT UP WITH A START, EXPECTING TO SEE A POLICEMAN.
IF YOU TRY TO LISTEN, YOU MIGHT FIND YOU'RE INTERESTED.
THE SPEAKER'S VOICE WAS VIBRANT WITH EMOTION.
SUDDENLY IT SEEMED TO HIM THAT THE MAN WAS SPEAKING DIRECTLY TO HIM.
...I HAVE BEEN IN YOUR PLACE. I HAVE KNOWN WHAT IT IS TO LIVE UPON A CRUST OF BREAD AND SLEEP IN STAIRWAYS...

REALIZE IT! STILL IN THIS CITY TONIGHT...
...WOMEN ARE DRIVEN BY HUNGER TO SELL THEIR BODIES. MEN ARE WILLING TO WORK, YET STARVING...
...CHILDREN AND OLD PEOPLE ARE CAST OFF AND HELPLESS.
NOW TURN THE PAGE WITH ME, AND GAZE UPON THE OTHER SIDE OF THE PICTURE. AT THOSE WHO SPEND HUNDREDS OF DOLLARS FOR A PAIR OF SHOES...
...MILLIONS FOR YACHTS AND AUTOMOBILES. AND YOU PLOD ON LIKE BEASTS OF BURDEN, THINKING ONLY OF THE DAY AND ITS PAIN.
IS THERE ONE AMONG YOU WHO BELIEVES THAT SUCH A SYSTEM WILL CONTINUE FOREVER?
THESE WORDS WERE LIKE THE CRASHING OF THUNDER IN HIS SOUL.
WHO DO YOU EXPECT TO FORGE THE SWORD OF YOUR DELIVERANCE?!
THAT HE SHOULD HAVE SUFFERED SUCH OPPRESSION WAS BAD ENOUGH-- BUT TO HAVE SUBMITTED...
THE TASK IS YOURS. YOURS TO DREAM, YOURS TO RESOLVE, YOURS TO EXECUTE...

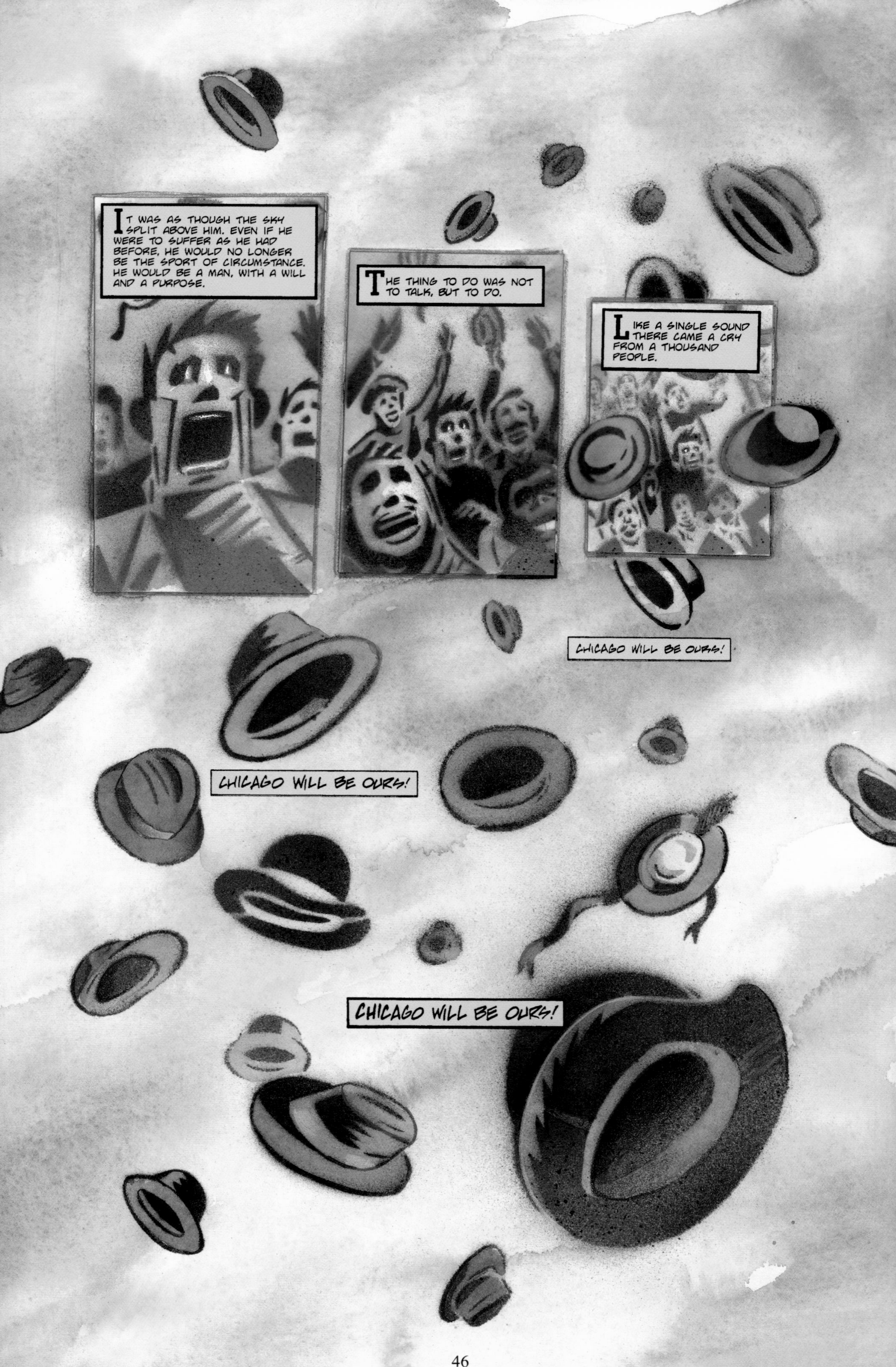
It was as though the sky split above him. Even if he were to suffer as he had before, he would no longer be the sport of circumstance. He would be a man, with a will and a purpose.
The thing to do was not to talk, but to do.
Like a single sound there came a cry from a thousand people.
Chicago will be ours!
Chicago will be ours!
Chicago will be ours!

Upton Sinclair was born in Baltimore in 1878 and was raised in poverty. His life as a writer began when he was 15 with the dime novels he turned out to pay his way through the College of the City of New York. He progressed to more mainstream fiction and produced six novels while enrolled as a graduate at Columbia, among them *King Midas* (1901) and *Manassas* (1904). These early works were not well received by the book-buying public and Sinclair earned very little from them; it took the publication of *The Jungle* in 1906 to assure his literary and commercial success. Perceived as a muckraking expose of the meat-packing industry, *The Jungle* was in fact written to advocate socialism. Sinclair, who had become a socialist in early life, used his royalties from the book to found the Helicon Home Colony, a prototypical socialist cooperative in Englewood, New Jersey; the experiment was abandoned after a mysterious fire in 1907. In 1915, Sinclair moved to California, where he unsuccessfully ran for governor four times, coming closest to election in 1938 when he forged the state's progressive elements into the EPIC (End Poverty in California) coalition. The campaign was acrimonious - his opponent was backed by the entrenched business community - and Sinclair was narrowly defeated. His activism was also expressed in such books as *The Metropolis* (1907), about morality in a society controlled by wealth; *The Profits of Religion* (1918), which espouses the viewpoint that organized religion is a capitalist tool for keeping the masses in their place; and *Boston* (1928), based on the executions of the anarchists Sacco and Vanzetti. In 1940 Sinclair published *World's End*, the first in a series of 11 novels starring the character Lanny Buddand covering international politics from 1913 to the height of the Cold War in 1953; one of the books in the series *Dragon's Teeth* (1942), was awarded the Pulitzer Prize. In addition to novels, Sinclair wrote short stories, plays and pamphlets, and has over 100 works to his credit. He continued to write into his eighties; the novel *It Happened to Didymus* was published in 1958, and his autobiography appeared in 1962. He died in 1968.

Peter Kuper was born in 1958 and grew up in Cleveland, Ohio. He moved to New York in 1977 and attended Pratt Institute. In 1979 he co-founded *World War 3 Illustrated*, a political zine, and remains on the editorial board to this day. He has taught courses in comics at the School of Visual Arts in New York City since 1986 and since 1988 has co-art directed *INX*, an editorial illustration group syndicated through the web at www.inxart.com. His illustrations appear in magazines and newspapers around the world including Time and The New York Times as well as Mad where he has drawn *Spy vs. Spy* every month since 1997.

He has written and illustrated numerous graphic novels including *The System, Stripped, Comics Trips, Eye of the Beholder, Mind's Eye, Speechless* and *Sticks and Stones*. His other adaptations include Franz Kafka's *The Metamorphosis* as well as *Give It Up!* collecting nine Kafka short stories. More of his work can be seen at www.peterkuper.com.

Peter wishes to acknowledge a number of people who made this adaptation possible. First and foremost, Emily Russell, whose tremendous efforts in co-adapting the text made this daunting process a pleasure, Wade Roberts for initially giving me the opportunity to do this project as well as a number of people at First Publishing for helping to see the book through all its stages, Ken Levin for being such a stand up guy, Terry Nantier and Martin Satryb for presenting it so beautifully, Tomm Scalera for stencil cutting, Willie Shubert for lettering and Ryan Inzana for production assistance. As always, thanks for the love and support of my wife, Betty and all of my friends and family. Finally, thanks to Upton Sinclair, whose work has been a guiding light--demonstrating so powerfully that art can be used as an instrument for change and benefit so many in the process.